TABLE OF CONTENTS

At the age of 64, I feel I am qualified to write my recipe for overcoming the abuse of the first 18 years of my life. I escaped to a happy, successful, and prosperous life, and believe that with the right attitude, a willing spirit, and a little courage, anyone else can, too. If I could do it, so can YOU.

When I was about 12, a book first planted the seeds of freedom in my mind. I hope this book will plant ideas that will grow to help others escape from their emotional jail and become happy, independent, and prosperous, as well.

CHAPTER 1
What, For Whom, & Why

(Because no one reads a preface)

INTRODUCTION:

Verbal abuse is a very cowardly and insidious strategy one person uses to control another. It is particularly cruel when the perpetrator is a mother abusing her daughter, which was my particular situation. When a daughter is programmed with years of belittling and berating by her mother, the person in her life with the most "natural power" anyway, the emotional injury is especially deep and lasting. But all verbal abuse has a devastating effect on its victim.

I am presenting a new perspective on the situation and hope that verbally abused daughters, and anyone abused in any way, can gain personal strength and support from my practical, down-to-earth approach. This is not simply a theory conjured by someone who has never experienced abuse, but a new perspective from someone who has "been there" and escaped.

WHAT:

By title, this is a book written to help YOU overcome verbal abuse. I have intended it to be a practical guide to discovery, realization, understanding, and healing of the psychological wounds inflicted by the verbally abusive programming of anyone important in your life. (Naturally, if they aren't important to you, their verbal abuse would not be significant.) I specifically speak from my own experience, which is the most deeply set type of verbal abuse: that of a daughter raised by a verbally abusive mother. Whether your abuse came (comes) from your mother, father, sibling, spouse, or any other relationship in your circle, I hope you will be able to identify with my experiences, find comfort that you are not alone, and enhance your life by ridding yourself and neutralizing the effects of this toxic relationship.

This guidebook is intended to help anyone verbally abused escape from the psychological jail in which they live. Once you realize that your abuser has gained emotional control over you by putting you in an emotional jail that limits your independence, you can begin to take steps to take control of YOUR SELF and attain emotional freedom. And once free, you will not want to pass on this abusive behavior to your own children or others. A strange phenomenon to me is the fact that most ABUSED individuals become, themselves, ABUSORS. I believe this is

4

because they have not been able to heal themselves, have not recognized verbal abuse for what it really is, have made excuses for their abuser, and have thereby accepted the abuse as a right of parental authority. Consequently the disease spreads to the next generation.

This book is intended to give you a new point of view from someone who has "BEEN THERE", has tried the psychologists' approaches, (which I believe perpetuate the practice of abuse), and has developed my own view of the problem. "If I knew then what I know now", it wouldn't have taken me so long to get "HERE", to happiness. Maybe the experiences and ideas presented here can help YOU achieve healing sooner. It worked for me.

As I have written the later chapters, I have returned here to add that I really view this ensemble of suggestions as a "recipe" for healing verbal abuse. As the chapters progress, each one adds various ingredients, both tangible and intangible, that I have found to be essential elements towards final resolution of verbal abuse. As with any recipe, you may want to omit some of the ingredients or add some of your own to spice it up, but the purpose of this book is to be a practical guide and at least a starting point for your future-free-of-verbal-abuse, and amelioration of its affects on your self-esteem.

FOR WHOM:

I am particularly speaking to women ages 14 to 100, who have been the victim of verbally abusive mothers, which was my situation. However I think any abuse victim could benefit. **It's never too late to wake up and enjoy your existence!** This book would probably be helpful and useful to anyone who has been verbally abused, or suffered any other sort of bullying, since these are all situations where one power figure dominates another through the use of language and "abuses" their power, thus trapping their victim emotionally.

YOU KNOW you're not "worthless", "good-for-nothing", or, as my mother used to refer to me: "a no-good skunk" or a "dirty rotten louse". You read the books on self- esteem.   You logically fight against succumbing to this vicious programming. But then you stumble; perhaps it's an argument with your loved one or perhaps a cruel remark by a child or an associate. Perhaps a stupid mistake you make, or an unfortunate remark. Often it doesn't take much to start your emotional spiral back to GROUND ZERO. *"Maybe my mother was right. I am worthless. Why else would SHE have ever said such awful things to me over and over again? She was right. I am good-for-nothing."* Etc, etc.

It all comes back to haunt you at weak moments.

   I hope this book can help you learn to respond to those occurrences with a quick emotional reflex action back to your normal, happy state of self-esteem. It is not easy, but if I could do it, so can YOU.

WHY:

When I was going to have my child, at the age of 36, I was hoping to have a boy. I did not want to relive the relationship I had with MY mother again! Everything I had read indicated that this type of behavior is usually passed along through the generations of families. Children of divorced parents are more likely to be divorced themselves; children of abusive parents are usually abusers themselves. I was in luck, however, since my husband's family usually had more boys than girls. The odds were on my side. THEN IT HAPPENED!! The amniocentesis test revealed that I was going to have a girl!! I decided right then that my relationship with my daughter would not be a replay of my relationship with my mother. I TOOK CHARGE.

I only began to realize others might benefit from my own healing when I met a fellow employee in the ladies' room at work one day. After congratulating her on the news of her pregnancy, she expressed to me that she was hoping it would be a boy. I immediately countered, saying I had hoped for a boy, but was very delighted with the fun I had been having with my daughter, Katie, and was now glad I had had a girl instead!! She proceeded to tell me that because of the lousy relationship she had had with her own mother, she did not want a girl, fearing she would have to relive the mess again with her own daughter. Needless to say, I was astounded that ANYONE FELT THE SAME WAY I HAD FELT!! Naturally, I told her of wanting a boy, of my own anxieties at learning I was to have a girl, then of the wonderful love and fun I was experiencing with my own daughter. I told her that SHE could define the relationship she would have with her own daughter, just as I had done.

Well, guess what! She had a girl, was having so much fun she quit her job to be a full time, old fashioned mother, and the last time I spoke to her, she was having loads of fun and a very loving relationship with her little girl.

Over the years I have met many women, both older and younger than myself, who have carried the emotional scars inflicted by lousy mothers. This book is being written to help primarily verbally abused women, but also women who have had a lousy mother or anyone verbally abused:

1) See verbal abuse as what it is, cowardly control, NOT the right of an authority figure.

2) Realize that there is no excuse for verbal abuse

3) Recognize their emotional scars and take steps to heal them
4) Escape from their psychological jail and from the limits programmed by the verbal abuse
5) Refuse to be a victim of abuse
6) Refuse to practice any abusive behavior
7) Take better care of YOUR SELF and your self-esteem

I hope my point of view can help others overcome the devastation of abusive programming and improve the quality of their life and that of those around them.

CHAPTER 2

STEPPING INTO THE LIGHT

(Or how a change of perspective improved my view)

I thought I was doing very well. It was 1984; I had two Masters Degrees, a husband, a career, a dog, and now a little daughter. Not bad for a no-good skunk who doubles as a dirty rotten louse who is worthless and will never amount to anything ! (According to my mother).

Anyone brought up or living with verbal abuse of any kind knows the scene, but I'll summarize mine. Misery loves company they say, and I will admit that I found it comforting to come across others who had experienced the same habitual berating that I had. It's like an instantaneous camaraderie and mutual understanding. If you haven't lived with abuse you cannot truly realize the emotional entrapment, which is especially difficult to escape when it's programmed in during childhood by a parent or other authority figure.

I guess every abuser has their "pet" names and phrases; my mother would either call me "Barbara", "dirty-rotten skunk", "no-good louse", or "worthless good-for-nothing". From time to time she would threaten to send me to Saint Vincent's Orphanage, (wherever that was), and was sure I was not really her child anyway, probably being switched by accident at the hospital, since I was a brunette and my two subsequent brothers were blondes. (PS: she was a brunette!) When I made a mistake or broke something, I would hear about it for years, as she would use these examples during her nagging spells to underscore how worthless I was. Materially we were cared for, but my mother dominated the household with emotional control.

I felt however that I had conquered, as much as possible, the effects of my mother's verbal abuse, and there was no way MY daughter would be raised with that negative programming, nagging, and yelling.

I had taken several Psychology courses and read several books. The one that was most influential for me was Psycho-Cybernetics by Maxwell Maltz, when I was in my early teens. This was a major turning point in my life. To me the book said that I could succeed if I believed I could, that I could control my own mind, that I could take steps to overcome the past and control my own future. This, and an old book by Laura Spencer Hope, Self , planted the seeds of self-control and self-determination, that slowly germinated into branches of independence and flowers of success. VERY SLOWLY. These were really the beginning of my independent thought, which would progress to overcoming the years of abusive programming.

I had rationalized and "understood" why my mother indulged in verbal abuse. She didn't really want children, but after World War II women got married; they had children. She followed the norm, then found herself in the trap of motherhood. She must have felt frustrated, even jealous of a daughter who had her life in front of her. She had not wanted me to attend college; "Secretarial school was good enough for me; it's good enough for you.", she would say. She must have been even more frustrated with me, since I had become numb to her abuse, name-calling, and belittling. Working every summer and frequent babysitting during the school year was some escape. I even saved my earnings and put them together with a scholarship to attend college. All the literature and psychologists said, "FORGIVE". I "understood"; I made excuses; I rationalized; I forgave.

BUT STILL, there were situations when I would stumble in life, and then would fall back into that little depression. *"My mother was right! I am good-for-nothing! I'll never amount to anything. No one's MOTHER would say such things unless they were true!"* It was like a haunting, a disease waiting for the chance for your immune system to weaken, then it could race in and invade your well being.

Over the years I developed my emotional reflexes somewhat; "Wait a minute! Look at what you have accomplished. Remember SHE was just frustrated. You have done THIS, THAT, SOMETHING ELSE !! " But it always took time to bounce back. It was as if these abusive labels were always with me and from time to time they would take over again. Each time I would try to cover up my worthlessness with my education and my accomplishments, but I would never really escape from the abusive labels that had been programmed into my identity. They affected my choices in friends, men, and jobs, by never reaching too high and putting up with ill-treatment when I should have moved on. Life was okay, but I, myself, was still emotionally enslaved in this jail of limitations and low expectations, programmed in by the verbal abuse.

THEN IT HAPPENED!!!! One day I was playing with and talking to my daughter. She was just an infant, and I was telling her what fun we would have over the coming years. I told her how much I loved her. I told her I would NEVER call her belittling names like my mother did to me. I told her I would NEVER say such hurtful things to her.

THEN, LIKE A SUDDEN, STARTLING MENTAL FLASH, I realized how cruel a mother would have to be to say such hurtful things over and over.... over years.... to her own daughter!!!! How insidious and down right cruel a mother, or anyone, would have to be. I was actually shocked to think what a cruel, miserable, hateful, destructive character a mother would have to have, in order to verbally abuse her own daughter. I was amazed and stunned by the realization. It was as if a bright light had been suddenly turned on in the dark room of forgiving excuses, and I was able to see the cruel character I had been making excuses for and essentially defending over the years.

There are no excuses for any kind of

abuse to one's child. It is

unforgiveable....period.

The change in perspective, from that of a victim of a mother's verbal abuse to that of a mother myself, made me realize how vile and repulsive any such mother would have to be to perpetrate degrading verbal offenses on her own daughter year after year throughout her formative, vulnerable development. Especially a mother, the most powerful figure in any daughter's life, her role model, the person she identifies with in her early development. What a detestable, cold-hearted mother one would have to be, to belittle, berate, and humiliate one's own daughter....not once, but continually.

I was totally repulsed. I finally allowed myself to say it; I hated my mother. She was a miserable, cruel person. AND I FELT FREE AT LAST, vindicated. All those years of making excuses and feeling that I had to forgive her were over. **THERE CAN BE NO EXCUSE FOR VERBAL ABUSE.** It's an unforgivable way to raise a child.

I was amazed. I really felt as if a huge weight had been lifted, emotionally. It was like being released from a psychological jail. I was no longer a victim who felt obliged to make excuses for a lousy mother's behavior in order to prove to myself that I really did not DESERVE such treatment. There simply are no excuses whatsoever for berating your child year after year with negative programming. It is simply wrong. No excuses. UNFORGIVEABLE. Any verbal abuser, or abuser of any sort, is simply not a decent "mother". Any abuser of their own child is a sad example of cruel, hateful character, who is using their position of natural power over their child in a destructive and permanently damaging manner. UNFORGIVEABLE. For somehow forgiveness implies that the behavior is excused, tolerated, understandable, and therefore condoned. Now, as a mother of a little girl, I was able to see things more clearly, more objectively.

And with this perspective as a mother, myself, I realized that there are no pardoning excuses for verbal abuse of one's own children, (or other "loved" one).

And yet I still worried that I would become frustrated with raising a child as time went on and would fall into that unhappy pattern of name-calling and belittling to maintain control as a parent.

As my daughter got older, my new outlook only intensified. It seemed that I loved my daughter MORE as the years passed, and we had even more fun together. At some point I realized that I had succeeded in being the kind of mother I thought was correct, the kind I'd wished I'd had, not just a sad repetition of my own mother's abusive, cold style of parenting. The passing of abuse from generation to generation is NOT inevitable. Having experienced it myself, I simply REFUSED to repeat the behavior. Sure, the psychologists' studies indicate that one who has been abused is most likely to become an abuser themselves, but this is not necessary. (I believe the key is NO FORGIVENESS for the abuse you suffered, but I will address this later in more detail.)

I also did not want my daughter to be infected by such cruelty. I would never leave my daughter alone with such a person, even for a second.   In fact, I would not even want my daughter to come in contact with THAT kind of person. To this day my daughter has had no contact with my abuser. To this day we have a happy, peaceful home.

CHAPTER 3

STEP 1: START WITH THE HEART

(Or STOP making excuses for unforgivable behavior)

      This chapter will put forth a philosophy very different than any I have read over the years. Every psychological theory I have come across starts with FORGIVENESS. You are supposed to FORGIVE your abuser. You "have to understand" that they have problems, that they had a difficult life, that maybe they too were abused, that they have personality flaws, that they are under stress........whatever........you are to start with forgiveness. There is some strange idea that without this forgiveness of your mother, (or other abuser), you will be psychologically scared for life and that you cannot attain peace of mind over the situation. "They" reason that without this forgiveness, you will carry around an emotional burden that will eat at you, depress you, impede your healing. As I've described in Chapter 2, I did that for years. It sounds very sweet, very civilized, and it certainly is very kind to the abuser. The victim takes the benevolent approach and is supposed to be the forgiver. But the **victim** is the one making the accommodation, trying to reason WHY their oppressor has been cruel, and there is no resolution to console their heart.

WHY FORGIVENESS DOESN'T WORK:

To forgive anyone for any type of cruelty, you start with whether it was actually deserved by you. After all, your abuser probably doesn't treat everyone abusively. In my case, my mother adored my two younger brothers and would certainly not have even spoken to mere acquaintances as she did to me. Why? Why treat me differently? Evidently because I was not as good as others, not worthy of better treatment. This facet of the forgiveness philosophy is unconquerable for healing the heart, for even after you have tried to reason it all out logically, you are still left with the sadness that it was done TO YOU, by someone who is supposed to love you. If your abuser really cared about YOU, really loved YOU, despite their reasons, WHY be abusive to YOU? An abused daughter, wife, or whatever is hard pressed to hurtle this dilemma, for even if they think they have achieved a blanket forgiveness of their abuser, there will always be that little nagging question: if they loved me, WHY did they treat me so cruelly? Am I really worthless, good-for-nothing, etc? When problems occur in your life, the downward spiral is fueled by these underlying questions.

Victims are very resilient, however, and for myself, I spent years rationalizing that since I was a girl, my mother saw her lost opportunities more in my life that in those of my brothers, and therefore took her anger and frustration out on me more readily.   After all, on the path to forgiving abuse, you keep looking for excuses to explain LOGICALLY & UNEMOTIONALLY the cruelty someone you are supposed to love, and who is supposed to love you, has inflicted upon you.

YOU try to rationalize the behavior.

YOU look for excuses to benefit and forgive your abuser and heal your heart.

YOU try to "understand" their situation.

YOU can't really blame your abuser, because they
- a) have a problem
- b) had a difficult childhood
- c) are suffering themselves
- d) are under a lot of stress
- e) whatever

Your abuser has now these various excuses for having made your life miserable. You are supposed to forgive them, for you are a higher human being and more in control of your emotions. This might work with a casual relationship, but when love or especially a parent-child or spousal relationship is involved, it puts the victim's feelings aside to defend the actions of the abuser. In essence, the victim is placed below the needs of the abuser.

Forgiveness implies that the abuser is excused from fault, for they have these problems, these stresses. They have an excuse for the abusive language or behavior they lavished on you over the years. There is NO apology required to earn this forgiveness, making it seem that abusive behavior is a parent's right. (I can't tell you how many times people have said to me, "After all, she's your MOTHER.") By implication then, it was OK for them to abuse you now that you have a nice set of excuses to explain their cruelty. If you were in their place, perhaps you would have perpetrated the same abuse on your loved ones. Yes, maybe if you have a daughter, you would verbally abuse her just as your mother did you. After all, how could you help it if you had to deal with this problem or these stresses or that childhood? Your child would have to "understand", just as "they" say, and FORGIVE you, too. After all, you're her "mother". **STOP RIGHT THERE !!!!**

I was at this point, when I found out I was going to have a baby and it was going to be a girl!!!! Since I had all these excuses lined up for forgiving my own mother, would it be OK for me to perpetrate the same verbal abuse on my own daughter ?? Would I be able to control myself in those moments of anger and stress?? Would I find myself belittling my child, berating her with "you dirty rotten skunk" or "you worthless louse"?? I must admit I had a certain amount of anxiety about my future relationship with my daughter, but I really did not want to relive the yelling, nagging, belittling, and berating, even with me as the controller. I combated this anxiety with a firm resolve to be the kind of mother I had always wanted. I had always been rather independent; I reasoned: I am the one in control, NOT my mother. There is no law of nature that says I will be a duplicate of my mother. I am in control. As I described in Chapter 2, I didn't have anything to worry about.

There is such a thing as unforgivable

behavior.

Our society currently does not seem to agree though. There are excuses devised to explain everything from verbal abuse, to physical abuse, to delinquency, and even murder. Hell, I remember when graffiti vandalism in New York City was excused as "urban art", a way for the socially and economically oppressed to express themselves.

Well the CC subway line was certainly ugly and would only depress riders more. As long as you have some excuse or reason, society is supposed to "understand" WHY you did it. This implies it was OK for you to do it. And by implication, it is condoned. Sure you acted irresponsibly, but you had a reason, an excuse. That's how a society's values become changed. That's how abuse is handed down from generation to generation. That's why if you were an abused child, you are statistically more likely to be an abusive parent....(per my theory).

There is such a thing as unforgivable behavior. Verbal abuse inflicted on one's child is unforgivable. Of course, so is any kind of repeated abuse on anyone. It cannot be condoned. It is inexcusable. **A victim of abuse should not be forgiving of their abuser, for if you do not excuse it in others, you will not excuse it in your life, and you will not pass it to other generations. Only by recognizing abuse as unforgivable, can you really feel your heart is healed.** You did nothing wrong and there is nothing wrong with you. The abuse stemmed from the unacceptable, inexcusable, and unforgivable behavior of your abuser....no matter who it was. Abuse is cruelty towards another living creature, and that is simply wrong. When you recognize this fact and apply it to your abuser, you can finally realize that any abuse you experienced was NOT your fault, was NOT due to your actions, and was NOT something you somehow "deserved". There is nothing wrong with you, (although your abuser would like to have you believe there is; this gives her (or him) more control over you, after all.) She (or he) is the one with the problem.

Don't excuse it. Don't condone it.
Don't allow it in your life. Don't take it.
Don't practice it.

As I said in Chapter 2, the sudden realization of the cruelty it would take to verbally abuse, belittle, and berate your own daughter, made my mother a very despicable character in my eyes. I did not want such nastiness in my life or in the life of my daughter. I rejected it, and I finally felt a free, clean, clear conscience. I was not the one with the problem, I did not deserve belittling, and I had done nothing wrong. It was finally over, finally resolved, never to be relived again.

Now you're ready for Chapter 4. Forget it.

CHAPTER 4

STEP 2: CUT THE CRAP

(Or Don't waste time sifting through emotional

trash)

All right. You have realized that the verbal (or other) abuse in your life was wrong, that it was no fault of yours, that there is nothing wrong with YOU , and that your abuser, or in my case my mother, is the one with the problem. You do not have to make any excuses for your abuser and you do not have to forgive her (or him). You recognize verbal abuse as unforgivable. You do not accept it in your life and you will not practice or condone it. What's next?

My philosophy: Cut the crap out of your life. Eliminate the toxic people. Psychologists say "forget". At least we are a little closer on this point. As you will see, however, I take it a little farther.

DON'T FORGIVE THEM, BUT DO FORGET THEM, AND DON'T PUT UP WITH ANY MORE ABUSE. [1]

To forget someone is the most devastating punishment you can give them, for in your world

---

[1] If you are still living at home with your abusive mother, or are in for a substantial inheritance, read on, but stay tuned for a practical approach to this situation. After all, you don't want to end up on the street.

they no longer exist. They are emotionally banished, exiled. They no longer have any power over you or any place in your life.

ANALOGY:

In essence, you have been confined and limited by the psychological, emotional jail of verbal abuse. The erroneous negative programming your abuser used to control you, gave you a warped self-definition. *YOU could never do this or that, so you better not even try. After all, when you get right down to it, you're just a worthless..........., remember??* You are emotionally injured by this verbal abuse, and you have an emotional wound. The abuse which caused this injury is unforgivable. You have taken steps to prevent further injury by eliminating this toxic relationship from your life and are adopting healing attitudes and practices. You cannot expect this wound to heal rapidly, for you did not suddenly become wounded; this verbal abuse process occurred over time. But, <u>as you apply</u> <u>positive attitudes and actions to your daily life, a scab will form to</u> <u>protect the wound from further infection and eventually heal</u>. It will never heal if you continually "pick" at it with resentment, hatred, and mental regurgitation of the old abusive situations in your life. FORGET it, let it heal, and move on to build the future.

26

As time goes on and you concentrate on the positive aspects of your life and your future, you will think about your scab less and less. Soon, there will just be an emotional scar left. Leave it alone. FORGET it. The longer you forget about it, the more it will fade out of your life. Sure, that scar will always be there; once in a while it may itch or hurt a bit, but it will become increasingly diminished the more you occupy yourself with positive, forward-looking thoughts and actions.

A SAD PARALLEL:

I've known several women whose husband has left them for another woman. Some box up that emotional baggage, put it in storage, and work on forgetting it by going on to concentrate on the positive possibilities in their future. They work to heal the emotional wounds and often become more successful and happier than they were before the divorce!

Unfortunately I have known other divorcees who fixate on their divorce. Their emotional life becomes stalled at this very low point. They continually resuscitate their old marital problems, wasting their valuable energy on their old unhappy history. In other words, they waste even more time on this bum who doesn't deserve a second thought.

27

Why carry around useless, burdensome, emotional baggage? It doesn't do you any good. You cannot move ahead carrying around a lot of emotional garbage. It won't change the past. **But it will cripple your future**, for parallel to verbal abuse, you must learn from it, FORGET it, and apply your efforts to positive, healing activities and thoughts.

HATRED DOESN'T HELP:

Hatred, anger, and thoughts of revenge are all included in crippling emotional baggage. You should not even waste ONE THOUGHT on these people. Forget about your unfortunate abuser. Yes, I said "unfortunate abuser"! By recognizing their abuse as unforgivable and with no further power over you, by forgetting them, you leave them "an abuser with no victim", or at least with one less victim. They know what they have done, but don't expect them to admit it. Life is too short. Your energy is too valuable. Use it for your family, your friends, your future, and, most important of all, YOUR SELF.

FORGET AND MOVE FORWARD:

Looking at the situation from the outside, it's easier for one to see the sad self-torture and masochism of someone literally "going back for more". Why subject yourself to the same painful emotions and memories? Stop wasting your valuable time. Stop poisoning your life with these old toxic situations and memories. Forget them, move forward positively, and don't look back. I don't know who said it first, but truly **"THE BEST REVENGE IS LIVING WELL."**

LIVING WITH ABUSE (TEMPORARILY):

Now I'm a very practical and realistic person. There are some circumstances which might require you to put up with the verbal abuse for a certain amount of time. (Get help as soon as possible if you are experiencing physical abuse!) Let's address this.

It may be necessary that you live with verbal abuse for a temporary period of time. If you are a teenager living at home with a verbally abusive parent or a wife married to a verbally abusive husband, you probably will not be able to make a quick, clean break from your current situation. It is easy to list ideal steps to take, but practical reality is that you may be economically restricted for a while. It would be reckless to take any action that would leave you "on the street." One has to be practical.

29

As I mentioned previously, when I was in my early teens, my exposure to Maxwell Maltz's book Psyco-Cybernetics and another book by Laura Spencer Hope about the Self greatly affected me. We lived in the woods of Westchester County, so I had lots of time alone to read and think. I believe my independent thinking grew from these literary seedlings. One's mind is a wonderful resource, but I don't think most people use it. Instead they take the easy route of passive thought, essentially nodding and going along with life as presented to them.

Your abuser has effectively programmed you to believe that you are worthless, good-for-nothing, stupid, ugly,....whatever. Once you are able to

- Recognize this verbal abuse

- Realize it is a cowardly, insidious power or control technique

- Regard it as unforgivable

- Recognize how limiting your emotional jail is and that you can only be so confined IF YOU CHOOSE TO BE

I believe you can begin to heal your emotional scar even if you are temporarily economically tied to (live with) your abuser.

Whether you are a teenager at home or a wife without resources, I believe you can establish a mental strategy and take steps to prepare yourself for economic independence. Once you realize that only YOU can control your mind, "no one can make you feel inferior without your permission." (Eleanor Roosevelt quote) Things may be said to you, but they will no longer have the power over you, as before. It actually is very empowering to realize you have a true shield against these attacks, and though you may not yet be able to actually assert yourself, you are none-the-less the winner of this power struggle. You can make your move by escaping to college, as I did. Throughout high school I worked every summer, baby sat on weekends, saved my money, plus earned a small scholarship for college. There was also the benefit of extra time away from the nagging and negativity at home. But whatever your plan is, physically distance yourself as soon as practically possible. Only then can you permanently eliminate the abuser from your life.

Once free mentally and economically independent, you complete the coup by forgetting this person, they no longer exist. You have annihilated them from your world. Not possible you say? Oh yes, it is. I cut off my mother forever and after years last saw her in 1973. She stupidly still thought I could be manipulated, but of course she was wrong. I rid my life of that plaque forever, and it (she) was never able to infect my family.

There are so many positive people to be with, so much to accomplish in life, so many ways to have fun, just get rid of the emotional baggage, toxic people, and past garbage that can slow you down and trip you up.

CHAPTER 5

Abuse Is Not An Excuse

(Pain is inevitable; Suffering is optional)

Frank Fusina listens to people's problems all day, every day. He is a hair designer and colorist. His clients include men and women whose careers range from housewife, to movie star, to Senior Vice Presidents of major corporations, and to me....for over twenty years. Frank once told me something that has embedded itself in my mind. He stated how sad, wasteful, and ridiculous he felt it was that so many of his clients would tell him that they couldn't do this, or didn't do that, or weren't something more because of the way their mother (or father) treated them as a child. Their parents can be long gone, yet they still carry their past abuse around as an excuse for their own lack of initiative.

Once you're over 18, you can live your own life. But you can restart, retrain, redesign your world at any point. It's never too late to start a new project. Mieux vaut tard que jamais. Better late, than never. Today many people have HAD to start a new career due to corporate lay-offs, job consolidation, or job obsolescence. I, myself, have been a teacher, an auditor, a Director of Finance at a major entertainment corporation, and now a writer. If I can do it, so can you. Remember, I started out as a no-good skunk and a rotten louse who was worthless and would never amount to anything !!

After FORGETTING the abuse, you are in charge of your life. YOU make the decisions. YOU devise your own goals and plan. YOU take action.

Using past abuse as an excuse for your current predicament is like waving a flag of surrender to the past abuse. You gave in and now proclaim the power of your abuser's verbal attacks still dominates your life. They won; you won't think for yourself; you are living up to the belittling remarks. Probably you feel sorry for yourself. After all, look what a martyr you are....going on the best you can, considering all you've gone through! What a burden to have to carry through life!

Yes, what an emotional burden! Well, you know what I think you can do with your emotional burden....throw it away along the road of life. Refuse to carry this negative emotional baggage any longer. Every time you use past abuse as an excuse, you roll up your sleeve to show that old emotional scar. See? Because of this old wound, I can't do this, I gave up the chance to do that, and I can't become what I want to be. (Now really, how absurd does that sound?)

If you're going to forget past abuse, going to throw it out of your life, you can't resurrect it at your convenience to explain your troubles. It isn't a crutch to lean on when someone points out one of your weaknesses. You don't need a crutch. You don't need an excuse. You are responsible.

Who is in charge of YOUR life, anyway? YOU.

Who is responsible for YOUR action, or non-

action? YOU.

INFLUENCE:

Of course, this past abuse had a great INFLUENCE on your life, on your personality, on your very being. Many things influence us over time, but a mother's verbal abuse and negative programming has profound influence. True. But this brings us right back to the beginning of this book! This abuse is unforgivable. You will not condone it, not practice it, and not let it be part of your life any more. To do this, you must FORGET it. Cut it out of your life. That means totally. Don't even use it as an excuse.

Take responsibility for your life, your actions, your SELF.

Don't let yourself be drawn back into the trap. Leave the trash in the dump and move on to a sweeter smelling future.

PAIN IS INEVITABLE; SUFFERING IS OPTIONAL:

I first heard this statement from a man who worked for me. He had a degenerative disease that was as yet incurable and it caused him to be in frequent pain. I don't remember the exact circumstances, but this statement was unforgettable. Despite his continual pain, he enjoyed his life fully and no one would have known his physical pain from his attitude and joy for living.

Everyone is going to have pain in their life. Some pain will be physical, some financial, some emotional. Instead of "suffering" under the burden of your pains, take action to eliminate the source from your life, and leave it behind. Be proactive. Take responsibility for your future. Concentrate on the positive aspects of your life. Take steps to bring closure to your problem areas.

Don't waste time sifting through this old emotional trash. Throw it away and FORGET it.

You don't need excuses for your past. You need a plan for your future. It does sound ridiculous for a thirty your old adult to say they never did this or that because of their mother's influence. So what's stopping you now?!?!

CHAPTER 6

Moving On !!

Who Can Help ? When do I start?

How long will it take before my scar disappears?

OK. The abuse in your life is recognized. It is unforgivable; you don't have to make excuses for your abuser. You will not condone abuse, not tolerate it, not practice it in your life. You also will not use it as an excuse. You will forget it. So where are you?

THE SECURITY OF JAIL

You often hear of criminals who are more comfortable in prison than out in the world of freedom. The psychological jail in which verbal abuse confines you can be even more comforting. The limitations that this emotional control puts on your actions are convenient excuses to avoid the risk required to pursue opportunities and self-development projects that could lead to success (or failure). *"After all, why should I try this or that, it (I) will never amount to anything anyway. I could never be this, and I could never do that. I'm just not good enough. It's just not ME. I would probably just fail,*

38

anyway." If there is ANY chance of failure, you have been programmed to be sure you will fail.

You may have developed a "learned helplessness", in the sense that you have been programmed not to assert Your Self, not to develop Your Self, not to think outside of the emotional jail your abuser has spent so much time programming you into. The last thing your abuser wants is to loose control over you. THE MOST IMPORTANT THING FOR YOU IS TO BECOME YOUR OWN PERSON, not a persona dictated to you.

Once you realize your situation and recognize that these limitations are WRONG and INCORRECT, once you recognize that all the verbally abusive programming was just a coward's attempt to control you, you can step back and look at your self-definition more clearly. Isn't it time to start being YOUR SELF and not just the verification of an abuser's cruel belittling? Life is short. Live it. Don't just hide in your emotional jail, waving the surrender flag of abuse, watching others maximize their life.

You CAN escape your psychological jail by simply stepping outside the arbitrary and ridiculous belittling boundaries of the verbal abuse.

Only YOU can do this however. There is no "Prince in Shining Armor" who will come. Don't bother to wait to be rescued. Only you can do it.

Sure, it takes guts to try. And it requires even more courage for the verbally abused individual. I know you have that emotional scar. But remember:

IF you don't try, you won't get.

IF she can do it, you can too. Just get the right training.

IF YOU don't go for it, no one is going to hand it to you.

IF you don't enter the contest, you will never win.

So don't just sit there, confined in your emotional jail !! Start to plan your escape today. Sure you have an emotional scar, but everyone has some burden to carry. You only have one life. Live it. Move on!!

WHO CAN HELP ?

Fine. You are standing there with this emotional wound. It is time to take steps to help it heal. I have found that over time, there is only one person (on earth) you can really count on. There is only one person who will always be there for you and understand your situation. That person is YOUR SELF.

Think about it a minute. Who knows you better? Who cares about you more? Who understands your situation best? Who has a real interest in your well-being? Who will never betray you, never make fun of you, never breach your confidentiality, and never have that power of information over you. Over time, YOUR SELF is the only one you can really count on, your #1 best friend. It's time to start being nicer to your best friend. Develop YOUR SELF. Educate YOUR SELF. Plan for YOUR SELF. And most importantly, be kind and patient with YOUR SELF. You are in control and independent from now on.

START TODAY:

❖ Don't sit around waiting for someone to help

   you. You'll be old and gray, still waiting, and have

   wasted your life waiting!

❖ Don't look around for someone who "understands" your circumstances. You could look forever and never find anyone. You don't need anyone's pity. Besides, you already have someone who understands you....YOUR SELF. That's MOST important.

❖ Never think that "love" will be the answer to your lack of self-esteem; it may seem like it is for the first month or so, but you had better be strong to take any relationship's ups and downs. Chances are you won't find true, long-term satisfaction and self-worth through another until you are a whole, strong person on your own.

❖ Don't wait until "this" happens or until "that" is over. There will always be one delay or another.

"There's no time like the present." Don't keep

YOUR SELF waiting. Start to repair your self-

esteem now.

Of course, it is very scary to think ultimately you are ALONE in this. Surely there must be someone out there who will eventually come along and tell you how wonderful you are, who will make you feel loved and important. I, personally, do not know of a real life, lasting example in the thousands of relationships I have seen over my 64 years. Are you just going to sit there and hope someone comes along to solve your problem? Fat chance! But suppose you get lucky? Then what will you owe them? Who will be in control of your life? How long will it last? Stop shilly-shallying. Stop avoiding the solution. The time is now.

If you are ever going to overcome the effects of the verbally abusive programming of your childhood, YOU have to start TODAY to turn your back on that emotional jail, take steps to heal your emotional wound, and proceed into your future with sheer bliss, knowing you are free from further verbal abuse and in control of YOUR SELF.

HOW LONG WILL IT TAKE BEFORE MY SCAR

DISAPPEARS?

A mother's verbal abuse of her daughter is probably the most damaging and most difficult abuse to overcome. For a girl, her mother is (usually) the most powerful influence in her early life. Being a girl, the daughter would identify more with her mother. Verbal abuse by a mother negatively programs the daughter over her most formative and most vulnerable years. It is relentless and very effective. Consequently, the negative self-image programmed into the daughter is very strong. It has become a basic element of her self-image and self-definition.

This is the essence of what you must strive to change. You will be changing your self-definition to be more realistic, not based on the cowardly belittling ranting of your abuser. When things go wrong, when someone puts you down, when your loved one becomes angry with you, this emotional scar is highlighted as you fall prey to that old abusive programming. *"No wonder these things happen to you! You're worthless, after all. Your mother was right, otherwise why would SHE have called you a worthless good-for-nothing all those years? No matter how hard you try, you'll never really be anything else."*

By recognizing this verbal abuse as UNFORGIVEABLE and WRONG, you have taken the first step in rejecting it from your life; you do not condone it; you do not practice it, and you recognize that it has no validity in your self-image. Now you have to re-define your self-image, eliminating the abusive programming from your self-definition. Don't expect this to be easy. You learned one negative definition of YOUR SELF from your mother (or other abuser), now you have to TEACH YOUR SELF the truth. Gradually, as you realistically re-define YOUR SELF, and your self-image, your emotional wound will begin to heal. The more you build on your skills, your future, and YOUR SELF, the more your scar will slowly fade. As time goes by and you busy yourself with the positive things in your present and future, you will often forget you even have a scar.

Of course, you will have set backs. A relationship will become rocky, you become laid off, you have a car accident. No life is perfect. That's when you are most vulnerable to fall back to that old abusive programming. "My mother was right. I am worthless. Nothing but a........"

❖ Stop right there !

❖ Don't re-open that old emotional wound.

❖ Don't step back into that old emotional jail.

❖ Have a mental list of some of your accomplishments. Review them and realize (once again) that you are truly a valuable, vibrant human being with health, happiness, and success in your future.

Over time you will develop this EMOTIONAL REFLEX. Every subsequent lapse should trigger this reflex to snap you back to REALITY. Whenever you start to fall back into the old abusive emotional pattern of thought, you will eventually become more adept at bouncing back. This little mental EMOTIONAL REFLEX will help you reject the verbally abusive programming whenever it tries to trap you again. You will not allow YOUR SELF to be limited or trapped by this bogus information any more.

Half the battle is becoming aware of the trap. The other half is developing a healthy EMOTIONAL REFLEX to catch YOUR SELF from falling into that trap again. You've escaped from the emotional jail of verbally abusive programming; now you have to move forward and use your freedom to enhance YOUR SELF.

GET READY TO TAKE THAT FIRST STEP. It gets easier after that.

CHAPTER 7

Self-Audit and Inventory

(My MBA had to sneak in here somewhere!)

You can't develop a strategic plan without taking inventory of your current resources and reviewing your present situation. When you go over what you have to work with, it is very important to be realistic and fair to YOUR SELF. If you have made poor choices in the past, remember that we have finished with the past and are working on improving YOUR present and future. Don't be discouraged if you have a lot of work to do. Open your mind and enjoy the process. You can have just as much fun "getting there" as you will once you've arrived. Besides, life really is a continual learning and development process, (unless you are a stagnant pool....yuck!)

YOUR BASIC TOOLS AND HOW TO USE THEM:

You have all you need in one basic, compact, portable unit....YOUR SELF. If you are an average, sane human being, I believe you can help YOUR

SELF better than anyone else can. No one knows you better. You can think for YOUR SELF. You can "do it YOUR SELF". You are an adult. You are in charge now, (not your abuser). You tell YOUR SELF what to do. You are the boss. You are responsible for your future. You have a mind of your own.

What you think about YOUR SELF, the attitudes you have toward YOUR SELF, the confidence you have in YOUR SELF, what you expect of YOUR SELF, and how you take care of YOUR SELF, will all determine your future....NOT the belittling name-calling of your abusive PAST.

YOU MUST BE KIDDING ! WHAT DO I HAVE TO OFFER ?

As a worthless, good-for-nothing, or whatever nickname your abuser programmed into you, what could you possibly have that counts? Chances are you have a lot more going for you than your abuser does. They boost their egos by putting you down, which means they must feel insecure if their ego NEEDS a boost. They want to control you for their own purposes. They lack something that they want to manipulate you into providing for them.

So let's look at YOU....at Your Self.

CONCENTRATE AND BE GRATEFUL FOR WHAT YOU HAVE,
NOT WHAT YOU DON'T HAVE.

Everyone is going to have certain strengths and some weaknesses. No one is perfect, but you owe it to YOUR SELF to be the best you can be. Some improvements may take longer than others. You may fail at times. Big deal. Stay strong. Stay focused. Stay tough. Assess your failure. Try again. As Mort Leavitt, a Macy's executive I worked for years ago said, "There's nothing wrong with making mistakes, as long as you only make the mistake once." Learn from your mistakes and failures. A

49

Teddy Roosevelt quote I love is, "Show me a man who makes no mistakes, and I'll show you a man who does nothing." You can be safe, (learned helplessness), and do nothing in that emotional jail, or you can step out to freedom to define your own life. Calculated risks can produce great rewards and great happiness.

The first time my daughter invited a boy to her high school vice-versa dance, he said no. She came home crushed. I said, "Big deal. There are about 149 other guys in your class. Ask someone else." She did, she went, and she had a great time. If you don't try, you won't get. No one is going to hand you anything. You have to decide what you need, what you want, what is realistic, then plan how to achieve it.

INVENTORY:

Let's look in the toolbox (YOUR SELF) and check some of the more important personal inventory items. You have to decide your own path in life, but reviewing some basics often sheds light on circumstances we overlook in our daily stressful routines.

PHYSICAL:

❖ If you can see, hear, speak, walk, and talk, you have a lot more raw material to work with than many people, and a lot to be thankful for. But many very successful, happy people are blind, or deaf, or disabled. Take care of your health, appreciate it, and look on it as a very great asset in your inventory, for without it you have nothing.

❖ Be clean, neat, and you'll smell sweet. That goes for your body, your hair, and your clothes. When you take care of YOUR SELF, you'll feel better, both physically and mentally.   Next time you are out, look at the people passing by. Realize the impression they make if they are unkempt. It doesn't take much to comb one's hair, to wear clean, neat clothing. One of my pet peeves is dirty hair; even combed, it ruins a whole appearance. It really doesn't take much extra effort to be neat and clean, but the psychic benefits to YOUR SELF and the better image you project to others will be very rewarding. The hopeless feelings and low self-esteem resulting from verbal abuse may stop you from making the most of what you have. Don't be afraid to look your best!

Yes, don't be AFRAID to look your best. That may sound silly, but I believe people with low self-esteem take basically either one of two choices: being plain and calling little attention to themselves or being flamboyant to call lots of attention to themselves. Of course, a choice in the middle is best. Just be the best YOU possible, but don't be afraid to be just YOU. Looking like a "drudge" does not win sympathy over time. Looking like you crave attention (floozy) does not win friends over time either...at least not the kind of friends you need. Be YOU, but be the best YOU possible.

For years I wouldn't wear earrings larger than the size of a pea. Any time I tried on cute earrings, I felt self conscious; people would think I was trying to look "fancy" when I was really just a very plain type. I felt like a fool. Jewelry just "wasn't for me." It wasn't until I walked away from my own emotional jail, that I began to feel strong enough to "carry off" wearing normal jewelry.

I never wore make-up, but when I went to college my fantastic roommate, Gael, one day said I should wear some. She put eyeliner on me. I said it really wasn't for me, but she encouraged me to leave it on for the day. Long story short, I still wear eyeliner every day, and every day I remember how she cared enough about me to encourage me to be brave enough to improve myself.

Gradually, as you too walk away from your own emotional jail, you will begin to feel an inner strength, inner value, and self discipline that will empower you to be the best real YOU possible. It will take time and you won't be able to make sweeping improvements immediately. Start slowly, start with small goals, and you will gradually feel better and better about YOUR SELF.

❖ Don't let yourself become too overweight. I have a weight I will not let myself exceed. Think thin. Hold in your stomach. Refuse to gain weight. You are in charge of YOUR SELF. Praise YOUR SELF when you refuse a dessert. Say no to fried foods of any kind. It will be hard at first, but after a while you won't even miss them. Take charge of what goes in your mouth and be fussy. You are in control now. Set a realistic weight for YOUR SELF. Most real people are not meant to be "model-thin". I consider myself a sport model. There are ectomorphs, endomorphs, and mesomorphs. Don't fight nature, but do the best you can with what you have.   Stay away from crash diets. Just eat with moderation.

❖ Don't smoke. My Aunt George, (her real name was Bertha), said the biggest mistake she made in life was to start smoking in her teens. At the time she felt cool. Now she has to live with its effects on her heart and lungs, and quitting was hell. Quit sooner rather than waiting until it is too late. I was fortunate, always hating the smell of smoke and was too beaten down to even think I had a chance to be part of the "in" crowd anyway.

❖ I think anyone reading this book is smarter than to play around with drugs, so I won't insult your intelligence by suggesting you avoid them totally. They will become just another type of imprisonment. One great rule is to always be in control.

❖ Think about your other bad habits. As you become happier with your real self, you may want to take them on one at a time. But, remember to be kind with YOUR SELF, as well as patient.

EMOTIONAL:

❖ Be patient and kind to YOUR SELF and those around you. There may be a tendency to be jealous of others; they have had encouragement, parental praise and support. You have endured just the opposite. Life is not fair, but you have the inner strength to leave behind the toxic negative and move forward in a positive way. Tearing down others will not build you up or help you. You are trying to escape from the negative emotional jail of verbal abuse. Jealousy becomes no one. Don't sit and whine. Would you like to be around someone who "wallows" in self-pity? It gets very old after a while. FORGET IT. No excuses, remember? You may not always find your kindness returned, but when it is you will have made some very valuable friends. Having emotional stability and maturity is a fabulous asset that can help you overcome many difficult situations in life. Be glad for others' success, as you will want them to be glad for YOUR successes ahead.

ATTITUDE:

❖ A strong, positive attitude is another great asset as you approach any task or goal over time. Think about your approach and reactions to the people, tasks, and problems you encounter daily.

One day I was driving by a church and on their sign was a quote, "Happiness is a choice." It struck me because I had been preaching to my young daughter that there are things in life we must do. Also, there are two basic ways to do anything. You can piss and moan your way through a task and be miserable all the while, or you can realize that since it has to be done anyway, you might as well make the best of it and do it as cheerfully and with as much enjoyment as possible. Why waste ANY time being miserable if you don't have to? You are in control of YOUR SELF and can go through life happily or miserably. It's YOUR choice.

My daughter would come home from first grade and bemoan the fact that she had homework to do. She would complain for a while and I would finally point out that if she had just sat down and worked on it, she would have had it done already. It wasn't long before she became very efficient with her homework and was able to enjoy her evenings after school much more.

There really is great truth to that statement: "Happiness is a choice." Life is short. Why not enjoy every moment possible? You'll be more fun to associate with as well.

❖ Be grateful for what you have, instead of bemoaning what you don't have. There will always be someone who has more of this or a bigger that than you do. Appreciate the health and possessions that you DO have. Remember, some people do NOT have as much as you and would love to be "in your shoes."

❖ Add a smile to your wardrobe. It will make you look better than any other accessory. I think you will find it will also make you feel better. People will respond more positively to you. No one likes to be around a depressed sourpuss for long. The next time you go to the grocery store, notice how many people are smiling; notice your own reaction to those who are smiling and those who are not. It always amazes me how few people have even the hint of a smile. Remember, there are two ways to do everything, happily or miserably. Why not enjoy YOUR SELF while grocery shopping instead of being merely tolerant, (and probably merely tolerable). You may be surprised at the results and benefits as people react more favorably to you and to your requests. I find that when I have a problem with a product or a service, a smile and a softer approach to the store personnel gets me more than I often have asked for. I am probably one of the very few who has approached them in a positive manner.

EDUCATION:

If it weren't for my education, I would not be enjoying my current lifestyle and I would have missed some wonderful experiences as well. Education is the one thing NO ONE can take from you. It will last forever. Education can also be a help in building self-esteem. And no one can intimidate you with their degrees if you have your own.

Assess your current status.

If you still live with your verbally abusive mother, (which assumes you are in high school), concentrate on your academics. Don't try to "show her" by dropping out of school or by doing poorly. That just gives in to the abuse. Work to improve YOUR SELF, so some day your abuser will "eat her heart out". Once you realize what is going on, realize that the verbal abuse is wrong, incorrect, and cowardly, you will (probably) be able to use your internal emotional reflex to protect YOUR SELF. My own mother's belittling rantings were so predictable, they were practically comical after a while. Of course it still is difficult to live with the negative nagging, but when you are in high school and a minor, you need the safety and financial support of your parents. USE your abuser for all they're worth. Get the best education you can and get a job in the summer so you will be at home as little as possible. Build YOUR future.

Can't afford college? Start slow. Take a night course or two. Do well. You may be able to earn a scholarship. A woman who worked for me at CBS finally got her Bachelors Degree at age 47; it took her ten years because she had to work full time to support herself, but she was thrilled when she finally earned it. She then went on to get a Masters Degree!! If she can do it, so can you. Don't forget about scholarships, teaching assistantships, and dorm counselor positions. If you don't ask, you won't get. No one is going to appear out of the blue and hand it to you. Ask. Research. Pursue.

ASSET INVENTORY:

You probably have most of these basics already. What you haven't mastered or attained you can consider goals. No one is perfect. Without goals life would be pretty dull anyway.

Appreciate what you do have. Value your health. Don't belittle your accomplishments. (Leave that to your abuser!!) Be glad you have made it THIS far. You won't find your happiness in material possessions. Check out Christina Onassis. You will find it FIRST in YOUR SELF and then in the people and world around you.

If you have nothing else, you have your most valuable asset and your best friend, YOUR SELF, free, realistic, and ready to move forward.
Every day, be grateful for ALL you have, especially your health and your self-determination (freedom).

CHAPTER 8

But, But, But.........

(That's Easy for You to Say!!)

SO FAR....

You have recognized verbal abuse for what it is: a cowardly and insidious way to control and manipulate you. It is wrong. It is cruel. It is unforgivable. You have rejected it and will forget it, throwing it out of your life like you throw away any trash. You will not practice it. You will not use past abuse as an excuse, and you refuse to suffer over the past. Remember, like a love affair gone bad or any other emotional or physical injury, pain is inevitable, but suffering is optional; we will always move on and forward.

Although you are ready to step out of your emotional jail, you must also realize that there is a certain "security" in being psychologically limited. It is easy to wallow in the status quo. You could always wave the abuse excuse flag in surrender to the frightening and uncertain challenges along the path to independence, responsibility, and growth. But NO, NOT YOU. The successful may fail, but never yield. Go for it. What the hell. If you don't try, you won't get.

You know you still have an emotional scar, but forget it. Leave it alone, and it will heal. The more you rely on YOUR SELF, the more you develop YOUR SELF, and the more you appreciate YOUR SELF for what you already are and what you really can be, the more your scar will fade.

Now that you have taken inventory and realize all the assets you already have, you can begin to use these assets to develop your future.

OVERCOMING FEAR:

No matter how well you plan and analyze logically the path you want to take, stepping out of your old mold is hard. Oh sure, other people have done this or that BEFORE you, but they had advantages. *THEY weren't worthless, good-for-nothing, destined to never amount to anything. THEY had encouragement. THEY.........* Let's face it. What is the REAL difference between you and them? WORDS. Cruel and untrue words that were programmed into your self-definition by someone trying to control and limit you. Sure, some people have certain skills, but you can develop your own skills, too. It doesn't matter if you are a little off-schedule. Better late than never. Many, many people become most successful later in life when they finally learn what they really want to do.

Sure, it's easy to know WHAT you need to do. It's easy to plan HOW to achieve it. But the execution of a plan is the difficult part. The absolute worst hurdle is THE FIRST STEP. After all, if you TRY and FAIL on THE FIRST STEP, you will be doomed. Of course you could always just try again, but FEAR OF FAILURE is a tremendous obstacle to overcome, especially for someone who is worthless, a no-good skunk, a rotten louse, the village idiot....merely more words.

Whenever I was afraid to try something new, I would look around at the other people who were already doing it. Wait a minute. SHE is doing X. I know I'm smarter than she is. If she can do it, there's no reason why I can't do it, too. I can cite many examples of this. Once a guy brought over two horses so we could go riding......a cute guy. I had never really ridden but what the hell. I knew the principles. I had seen tons of cowboy shows on television. How hard could it be? I can tell you I did pretty well, stayed on, and he didn't know that I was scared silly. Another time, my husband and I were on vacation in Bermuda. They didn't allow rental cars on the island, so tourists had to take the bus, a taxi, or rent motor scooters to get around....while driving "on the wrong side of the road". I was standing there hesitating about motor scooter rental when two scooters rolled by: one driven by a little old man and the other by a little old lady. If THAT old lady could handle it, why couldn't I? We ended up having a ball scooting around that beautiful island at our leisure.

The next time you want to try something new and are unsure, check out who else is or has done it. You can use the same technique for almost any challenge you hesitate to take on. But remember: IF YOU DON'T TRY, YOU DON'T GET. NO ONE IS GOING TO HAND YOU ANYTHING. After all, what's the worst that can happen? Do your own little "Cost Benefit Analysis", (yes, again with the MBA). If you try and succeed, what are the benefits? If you try and fail, what are the consequences? Don't forget the intangible and emotional results. How bad would failure be....really?

Look at me. I gave writing a try with this book. If it gets published, I'll have succeeded. If it's not published, I will at least have learned a lot about the process, practiced my word processing skills, and missed a bunch of television programs. But, after seeing some of the junk that IS published, I figure I might still have a chance. If you don't try, you surely won't succeed.

RESPONSIBILITY:

OK. Get ready for a concept that is revolutionary in today's society: TAKING RESPONSIBILITY FOR YOUR SELF AND YOUR ACTIONS. It has become acceptable for one to excuse their actions by placing blame on all sorts of trauma and troubles in their past. The actions, no matter how horrendous, are supposed to be mitigated because THIS or THAT happened to the criminal in his/her past.

❖ The murderer was not REALLY responsible since he was under the influence of drugs.
❖ The child molester couldn't help himself, since he was molested as a child.
❖ The wife beater was down on his luck and depressed; he just took his frustration out on his wife, maybe even blamed HER.
❖ A man dies of lung cancer after smoking for thirty years and the cigarette company is to blame, (& pay).

What's next? A guy jumps off a building and the architect is to blame for making it too tall?

In the preceding chapters I have advocated that your abuser is RESPONSIBLE for their actions, whether or not she/he was also abused. There is no excuse for verbal abuse, any abuse. I am sure she did not enjoy being abused as a child, so why would she practice the same abuse? Passing on cruelty keeps it in your life. The past is over. Why maintain, foster, and propagate unhappiness in your life? Why blame the past for your PRESENT actions? IT IS OVER. FORGET IT.

You hold your abuser RESPONSIBLE for their abuse of you. Now you must realize that ultimately only YOU ARE RESPONSIBLE FOR YOUR PRESENT AND FUTURE. No one is going to come along and hand you happiness or success. YOU, YOUR SELF, are responsible for earning it. Take charge and take off from here.

SETTING GOALS:

Set some goals for yourself. You might as well get started right now. I advocate daily goals and long range goals. Neither should be set in stone however. Any corporate strategic plan must respond and change for industry and market dynamics. Your plans should, too.

I love lists. You may start with your list for the next day. When you complete a goal/task, cross it off and FEEL the accomplishment....no matter how small the task was. What you have not done, move to the following day.

You have to build up your self-esteem and your expectations of Your Self. Start with small goal lists, first for the next day. An example could be: Pay bills, Start taxes. Call @ phone bill. Make dinner. Trim roses. Do face mask (don't forget Your Self).

Then make a goal list for the next week. When reviewing what is still pending after a week, look at the items left.

Were there too many items?

Did unusual circumstances arise that took precedence over your goals?

Are there any goals you are avoiding? If so, why? Next week, tackle the avoided items first. Plan your attack on the "dreaded" task. Usually you will find that it will be easier than you feared. If you cannot get this one accomplished, try breaking it down into smaller steps if possible.

Be kind to Your Self. Maybe you are not quite ready for this goal yet. Only you know, but remember, keep moving forward. Don't allow Your Self to stagnate or wallow.

I used to avoid making calls to correct or inquire about a bill or a problem with a service. It was very difficult for me to assert myself at all. Abusers program you to acquiesce to their agenda, and that becomes your expectation of all relationships. As I forced myself to make these calls more and more, I realized that all the procrastination just made it MORE of a task. By staying polite and human on the telephone, I almost always was easily able to solve the problem successfully.

CHAPTER 9

Your Choices in Life

Your choices in everything are a function of your expectations. Those who have been beaten down by abuse, bullying, or other types of domination will have lower expectations of what they deserve and there fore will accept less and feel they have to give more, in any relationship.

You dare not reach for a choice that you do not feel you deserve. You may stay on the edges of society, not daring to try to join groups, not giving people the chance to like you, and limiting your opportunities in every aspect of your life...social, career, love, family, style, education, everything.

When I was a freshman in college, a popular guy asked me out. The girls in the dorm urged me to go, so I did. He was very nice, we had a good time, but when he called for a second date, I told him that I was not the type of girl for him, that he should be dating someone popular. He argued, but I could not believe that I was good enough for such a popular guy to date. I limited myself. I never did date anyone who was the kind of man I would even consider spending time with today. I simply didn't feel good enough for him. I could not step out of that unworthiness that had been programmed into me..

Realize that most of your choices in life have been affected by your confinement in the emotional jail of verbal abuse. Being psychologically limited by this warped, abusive self-definition, you probably expect little from life, from employers, from lovers, from relatives, from friends...You expect less from every aspect of life...even less from Your Self.

You may feel you are not good enough, or not as deserving as others, to be treated as well as confident people would be. Low self-esteem from verbal, or other abuse may result in your over-looking or making excuses for sub-standard treatment. Treated poorly on a date? No engagement ring, even a small one? Paid less than others for the same job? Given shoddy workmanship, products, or services by a vendor? No romance or respect in your relationships? When you have been psychologically beaten down, you may choose not to question others' behavior, ask for an explanation, or make any demands of others. If you expect little, you will get little. If you project weakness, you will be preyed upon and used. If you play the victim, you will become one yet again.

It is therefore important to be mindful of your choices. We've already talked about physical appearance, which is as important to your psyche as it is to how others perceive you. I've read that in the first six seconds someone has judged you in an interview. Having interviewed hundreds of candidates in my career, I believe it is an uphill climb to overcome that first impression if it is bad.

Let me make you mindful of other areas in which you should be aware of the decisions and situations you may get into. You should also evaluate your current relationships as well.

Your Approach/Attitude

With the belittling of your abuser as your background, you will probably find that you are either cripplingly reticent to try a new thing, meet new people, attempt success, and assert Your Self, OR you are defiantly bold, even in-your-face, in an effort to fight back, to stand up for Your Self with others, to defend Your Self. Of course neither extreme will bring success or happiness in the long run.

The reticence will make you miss opportunities in your work, career, daily life, love, and socially in general. In other words, "Why try? Bye." You will limit Your Self to minimal success and respect in all facets of life. You assume defeat before you attempt to succeed.

The defiant, aggressive approach might get you what you want in the short-run, but you will drive people away over time. People will simply avoid dealing with you.

Balance, moderation, in all things as they say, is the best long-run strategy, but it's not always easy to maintain, especially when we meet so many little challenges every day.

I think the best approach is to aim to be the kind of person YOU would like to deal with, the old golden rule: do unto others as you would have them do unto you. Be the person you would like to deal with.

Simple gestures like please, thank you, asking, not demanding, a smile, holding a door for the next person, just common courtesy, all go a long way. You feel better and you will be surprised at the kindnesses you receive in return...of course not from everyone.

I was on the Madison Avenue bus in New York City years ago, got on at 34th Street; at the next stop a rather shabby, elderly lady with a shopping bag was struggling to board the bus. We all waited. Then an older woman, the best dressed on the bus, got up and lifted the bag, assisted the lady, and paid her fare. I must say I was embarrassed. I should have done that; I was seated closer to the front. Lesson learned.

Putting forth a balanced, reasonable persona distances Your Self even more from your abuser. You have thrown away that past and now you can enjoy people, work, leisure, and every little aspect of life.

People you encounter will not always be pleasant or receptive, but you can only control Your life. As you navigate through time, you can collect the wonderful people you meet and avoid those who are not compatible with you.

Making a habit of a balanced, optimistic approach every day will distance you more and more from that abused persona, and you will grow into a more confident, happy person. You are developing, growing, improving Your Self, so appreciate the chance you have, the positive path you have chosen, and your developing inner strength.

People You Associate With

People are very influenced by their peers, those they choose to hang around with. Others will partially define you by your associations. If you waste time with losers, pessimists, manipulators, liars, and such, you will probably find you soon develop some of their unsavory traits and/or be taken advantage of by them. To quote Ben Franklin, "If you lie with snakes, you will be bit." When there are so many positive, fun people in the world, why waste your life on the negative??

The Stagnant Wallowers

You will find there are those who do not want to be happy. Perhaps they feel they do not deserve to because of their own demons or the burdens they carry, but there is a point where you must realize that no matter what you do, no matter how well you treat them, no matter how you encourage them, they do not reciprocate or get any happier. They continue to wallow. They may latch on to you, someone who they can easily dominate or lead or attach to. With a little, a very little kindness you may fall prey to their purposes. Whether it is for a short- term friendship or a long-term "marriage", you, the loved starved abused, will be perfect fodder for their purpose. You listen to them moan and groan about their life, but they never end up doing anything or making an effort to improve their outlook or circumstances. You cannot allow Your Self to be pulled into another negative relationship. You can feel sorry for them, but you cannot lead their life. You are not obligated to continually try to uplift someone who won't try to stand on their own. You have given up the crutch of feeling sorry for Your Self; do not let others pull you back down.

Liars

Then there are the liars. I had a friend for many years whose lies seemed to grow worse with the years, or maybe it was just I who gained more self-esteem. I realize that as I gained confidence in myself, I began to wonder why I had kept making excuses for her insulting treatment. We would make plans and at the last minute she would give me some excuse why she had to cancel...even a Christmas dinner!! Then a couple weeks later she told me what fun she had had doing X on that Christmas Day. I let it go at the time, made more excuses for her, accepted the insulting treatment. That was the old, weak me. As I strengthened My Self, I saw her treatment for what it was...just an abusive "friendship"; if some better offer came along, she would dump me with a cheap lie. She lied so much, however, she couldn't keep them straight. I no longer waste my time on this liar. This was just an abusive relationship that I have left behind in the trash.

Lovers

When you have been beaten down, you feel so glad that anyone treats you well, that anyone "loves" you, you do not dare endanger that "love" by demanding certain of your expectations be met. You accept their attention whether or not it meets the standards you SHOULD expect and accept.

A lover may win you over with attentiveness and consideration for a while, but if this degrades into using you for a maid, a cook, and/or a source of sex, please don't put up with inferior treatment. Don't put up with yet another abuser. Because no matter how hard you try to please them, you will only be feeding their ego and basically telling them by your actions that you accept the way they are treating you. You feel it's all you deserve. If you don't speak up, demand good treatment, and be willing to end the situation, to move on, they will continue to use you for their agenda. Nothing will change unless you voice your expectations and follow through if they are not met. You will just be stepping into another emotional jail, maybe better than the last, but still not healthy in the long run.

It is out of character for an abusee to think of themselves, to insist on better treatment, to be ungrateful for the little positive treatment they are receiving. Beware you don't gravitate to another abusive relationship. Sure, there may be moments of decent treatment, but you should be vigilant that any relationship you stay in is a give AND take...not a one-way street. Don't allow yourself to be taken for granted. Make sure your desires are considered as much as your lovers'.

Balance in all things. Your self-esteem will take years to grow, but little by little you will realize that you <u>deserve</u> to be treated well, with respect, and with reciprocal admiration and consideration. Don't trade one emotional jail for another.

Bosses

An overbearing boss is just another abuser. If you find yourself sexually harassed, receiving unequal pay for equal work, treated without respect, start looking for another job. You may choose to seek legal action, but you may not want to go through the stress, subtle retribution, and social isolation at work. It is a small world and other firms may view you as trouble. If you are career-minded, it may be easier to move on, again leaving your abusive boss in the dust.

I had one boss in New York who yelled at everyone except his little chickee secretary and a minority woman, whose work had to be picked up by the rest of us. I was there two years....too long.

In Hollywood I encountered sexual harassment and unequal pay, but I stayed in the job, rationalizing that it was convenient, that as department head, I would bring in my daughter on occasion. Of course, I should have looked for a better position, or I should have sued for equal pay, which would have been a slam dunk, since I had three profit centers in a major market and a man in a very minor Midwest market had one small profit center, had less experience, less education, and made double my salary.

It is hard for an abusee to stand up for themselves. If you cannot, look for another job. You may be surprised at the opportunities out there. The best time to look for a better position is while you are working. If you don't, you may regret it later, like I do. A friend has told me that a "good" job often holds you back from looking for a better one.

Manipulators

People who "play" you for their own benefit, who placate you ONLY to get something they want, despite the cost to you, people who do not reciprocate your contributions to a relationship, are basically using you for THEIR needs, desires, and convenience. Really, all of the above types are manipulators in a sense. These are not fulfilling relationships for you in the long-run, because only one side is being fulfilled...theirs. If you find yourself in one of these, step back and evaluate the situation.

—After associating with this person, do you feel happy or do you feel empty and drained?

—Are you angry with yourself for putting up with their treatment?

—Do you make excuses for their lack of consideration for you?

Everyone has an off day, but if you are in a relationship where there is no respect for your needs and feelings, then you are back in abuse.

The clever manipulator will throw you a bone once in a while or they may temporarily placate you if you complain, but a healthy relationship consists of equal give and take without one party having to demand or beg for consideration.

Warriors

Several factors make people warriors. They may be egotists, who think they know how the world should run and consider all others too stupid to agree with them. They may be someone who feels they have been dealt an unfair hand in life and are angry at the world. They may be a super manipulator, who feels they should be telling EVERYONE ELSE how to live.

They are always at war...with their employer, their government, any authority in their life, any entity that they deem a challenge to their personal power or authority...and usually they are also at war with themselves. They are their own worst enemy.

The warrior is so busy watching for challenges to their authority, that they neglect my number one rule for happiness, appreciation of all they have in their lives and for the people who are there for them...including you.

In love and friendship, these warriors are calculating. They don't want to commit too much, don't want to give too much, for that might compromise their "position" of power in the relationship. They would appear weak, maybe vulnerable, they could be taken advantage of.

You could be the perfect partner or friend, but the warrior will NEVER fully trust you with their heart or their true feelings.

There is a certain tension, seriousness, and/or unease about them, as they are always ready to go to war over any possible affront or other challenge. They are not the happy or light-hearted sort. They must always prove themselves and put down all perceived affronts to their position.

They can be charming when THEY want to be, but these people will not be an enjoyable companion. They must be in control and are always fighting to maintain that position. If they DO give in to a partner's desires, they will most likely display passive-aggressive behavior to punish you for your choice.

Fighters

This group may not have any problems with you, but they are in a self-made struggle with the world.

They differ from the terminally unhappy in that their unrest stems from a need for acclaim, for recognition, a need to stand out from the crowd.

They fight the system by pounding at it, instead of working with or within it for change. After all, THEY know the way things should be. The world is blind.

They are internally restless, not necessarily physically aggressive. They are unhappy with themselves, unsatisfied. They should be recognized for their wisdom, but they have no idea how to communicate effectively with the system.

Verbal banter is often their sword of choice. They are ALWAYS right, those who do not agree with them are either stupid, believe the WRONG ideology, or just haven't seen the same refraction of light as they have. (I find these are usually males.) They are more than willing to tell others how to think and act, if others would only listen.

They do NOT respect, and rarely consider, others' opinions, since they do not coincide with their own. "These people do not know what they're talking about, anyway." They certainly will not respect yours.
No one can sway them. They are too smart.

Narcissistic? Probably.

In my view, they are so busy with their continuous battles that they have little time to LIVE LIFE, that would be frivolous. That would put them on a level with everyone else, the mere mortals who do not see things as they should. BUT the world IS changed and improved by those who live every day to the fullest, engaging in the mundane to improve the practiced ideology of society. The little things and the little people are the atoms. You cannot change the chemistry of the whole without changing the atoms.

My point is that these fighters will always be suffering some internal turmoil that only they can resolve. The battle has become their life force. They are the Don Quioxtes, and it's lonely out there. They may be with you physically every day, but they are very lonely without the acclaim they seek and the recognition the world is just too ignorant to give them.

THE BEST DEFENSE

The best defense against all of these types is to build your self-esteem. Never give up on recognizing and valuing your worth. Be discerning, not desperate, in your search for relationships. Some work, some don't.

Remember, if you expect little, you will get little.

Make sure your relationships and business dealings have balance and equal compromise and respect. You deserve no less. Not everyone will like or work with you, but that's their right, and you do not have to like or work with anyone unless you choose to. Never TRY to make people like you if you sense they don't. Catering to someone, becoming virtually their servant emotionally, doesn't create a balanced relationship. You may do nice things for others, but if there is no reciprocity, don't fight the inevitable separation. Move on. Expend your time and energy on those who appreciate you.

Continue to count your blessings, be grateful for them, and work to enhance your education, talents, and personality. Improved self-esteem will follow.

Respect your feelings and realize that ultimately all abusers are manipulators and all manipulators are abusers.

As you strengthen Your Self with education, self-respect, and emotional growth, you will grow your self-esteem and be able to reject abusive situations of any kind.

CHAPTER 10

More Encouragement

The secret to success is to get back up one more time than you fall.

You know what to do. You know you have just as much potential as anyone else. You know you are taking steps to develop Your Self. In some ways you have an advantage in that you are more focused and ready to appreciate your freedom to lead your own life. But make no mistake; you will falter. It will take time, but you will recover faster from each set back, until you no longer allow a set back to even occur.

You already have the raw material. Now you must dare to use it, EVEN dare to fail. Of course you will have done your risk-benefit analysis before attempting anything of great consequence.

Step away from the old fear and start to LIVE life with passion, to actively participate, and to try new challenges.

Slowly, you will develop an inner strength. You will find the courage to believe in Your Self.

What if you just can't? What if it's all not working? Sit down and go over the logic again. Maybe go over the previous chapters. The first successful step came for me in high school when I looked at others in my classes and realized that I was just as capable as they were of doing X or Y, so why not try?! I often used this technique to en-courage myself, as I described earlier.

If you have to cry, do it. If you feel depressed, realize it. If you fail and feel like a big loser, acknowledge it. THEN stop, go over your growing inventory of assets, be grateful for all that you have accomplished so far, climb out of that emotional hole, and START YOUR ENGINE again. Look up, NOT down. The next morning, shower away all that psychological grime, and take up where you left off.

Believe me, it may seem like forever, but you will get exponentially better as you continue.
NEVER give up. If you do, they win. You are strong. You are YOU. You can be all you work for...but it will take work, self-reprogramming.

If I could do it, so can you !!!!

CHAPTER 11

In The End

Looking back, I realize how lucky I have been. Of course the constant berating was detrimental in that it created my low self-esteem, but my independent thinking made me brave enough to take small steps, one by one, toward freedom.

The books that fell into my hands were crucial catalysts. Already in high school I had steeled my mind to covertly reject the name calling. I knew the truth and didn't have to convince anyone else. My Catholic religion made me never feel alone. I could always ask for help or air my problems. Somehow that made a huge difference to me. We Catholics are fortunate that we have lots of Saints to call on as well.

Step by step I found people outside of my family to be more encouraging, helpful, and kinder. My Giant Step to college was made a lot easier because of my roommate Gael Douglas. I was never alone there either.

I continued to move ahead, always wanting to improve myself, BA, MA, MBA. There has never been one instance when I regretted dumping my toxic mother. I actually celebrate the fact. It taught me to reject other toxic people I came across. There are so many wonderful individuals in the world, I never waste my precious energy on the users, the phonies, or the manipulators. I am always ready to help a friend, however.

And what of my two brothers and younger sister who were controlled?? About twenty five years later, my aunt in California got in touch with me (on my mother's orders) and updated me on my family. I also gave her an earful. My mother wanted to know what I looked like and what kind of a house I had. We concocted a doozy of a story that I lived in a dump with an old sofa on the porch and a broken down car on the front lawn. We concluded that if she thought I had money, she would probably pester me. I was DONE with all that. My brothers got college degrees as expected of them, but ended up living with and supporting their mother. They never married. Craig, the one I was close to, committed suicide at age fourty-seven; he had never married, and his mother chased away any girlfriends, per my aunt. My other brother became a copy of my mother it seems. My sister married, had three children, and works in a grocery store.

I continue to read books on self-improvement, the brain, and even a little quantum physics, so more idea seeds are always sprouting in my brain.

I am always busy with some little project or other and love people watching. I smile and talk to everyone. If they don't smile back, that's their loss.

I never make fun of or belittle others. Everyone deserves dignified treatment by those around them.

I appreciate and am grateful for every day, every kind person I meet, every experience and every little pleasure.

If we never experience hardship, we will never really appreciate our freedom, blessings, and earned rewards. Navigate around the torpedoes you encounter. Your abuser was one, of course, But we all will run into people who do not want us or anyone, to thrive. People who give constructive criticism and suggestions may be trying to help you, but those who are constantly negative about our ideas and dreams are probably jealous they have none. You do not need everyone's approval, and let's face it, you would never get a consensus anyway.

There is a basic dilemma in life. You must decide if you would rather wish that you HAD or wish that you HADN'T. Rather wish that you HAD and ponder your potential loss, or wish that you HADN'T and learn from your mistakes. I agree with Admiral Farragut, "Damn the torpedoes, full speed ahead."

In the end, I love life, and I consider myself to be the luckiest of our late family, because I escaped and vowed I would never live like that again.